PAUL NAYLOR

BOOK OF CHANGES

Shearsman Books

First published in the United Kingdom in 2012 by
Shearsman Books
50 Westons Hill Drive
Emersons Green
Bristol
BS16 7DF

Shearsman Books Ltd Registered Office
30–31 St. James Place, Mangotsfield, Bristol BS16 9JB
(this address not for correspondence)

www.shearsman.com

ISBN 978-1-84861-199-3

DATE DUE

			PRINTED IN U.S.A.

JAN 0 4 2013

Also by Paul Naylor

Poetry

Playing Well With Others (Singing Horse Press, 2004)
Arranging Nature (Chax Press, 2006)
Jammed Transmission (Tinfish Press, 2009)

Literary Criticism

Poetic Investigations: Singing the Holes in History
(Northwestern University Press, 1999)

The whole
is for D
my favorite
reader

Contents

This is the heart of the *I Ching*:
the breaking in of another view,
over which we have no control,
of which we understand little,
but which asks us questions
and puts us in a position of listening.

—Martin Palmer—

The poems in this book grow out of an extended encounter with the ancient Chinese book of divination, the *I Ching* or *Book of Changes*, which is a collection of sixty-four hexagrams comprised of various combinations of broken (*yin*) and whole (*yang*) lines.

The *I Ching* is frequently divided into two sections—the first thirty hexagrams and the final thirty-four hexagrams, known as the "Upper" and "Lower" Canons respectively. The first two series of poems in *Book of Changes*, in which I work through the hexagrams in chronological order, constitute a dialogue with those two sections. As for their occasions—my mother's death and, eight years later, my father's descent into the underworld of Alzheimer's disease—they arise from the listening grief assigns. Once we've asked all the old questions—why? what follows?—there's little to do but listen. Most of our models in the West teach us not to listen to nature when death arrives, so we listen for a voice beyond nature, something or someone standing outside and presiding over the perishing world we see and breathe in. The models of the East, of which the *I Ching* is among the earliest, suggest we listen to, rather than beyond, nature.

In "Limbic Knit," the third series in *Book of Changes*, I returned to the sixty-four hexagrams of the *I Ching* to accompany me through the gestation, birth, and early months of our daughter's life. That event and the others that compose *Book of Changes* have awakened and deepened a perspective I take to be true: a person is not a piece of eternal private property, sealed off and saved from the impersonal forces of nature. A person is a part of, not apart from, nature. The *I Ching* informs us about what, not who, we are—energy ordered by chance and necessity in an ongoing process where everything and nothing is lost. That's the other view that broke through as I listened, and what little I understood became these poems. Fragments they are—but fragments of a whole unassigned in advance, unfolding as change arranges us in its wake.

UPPER CANON

in memory of my mother

The Creative

sky above and sky below
a bird flies between time
its form marked for memory
though hidden the first cloud
contains the last we know
this way soon descends

The Receptive

earth beneath earth
the constant brings
forth from its belly
ten thousand things on
each side of the abyss
begin to ascend

Patience

hawk cuts west
across the river
clouds darken the sky
wait on this side
heard it said
somewhere

Disagreement

darkness sets light
aside as the vault
filled and covered
memory floods my life
with the fact not
the thought of it

The Army

of the dead from
whom we hear so little
water runs below the
earth's surface washing
recollection away of
what once was her

Unity

pine boughs bend
beneath snow's weight
white balanced by green
shadow by light
between the two is
one I understand

Restrain the Lesser

wind from the southwest
blows above the tree line
turning east against
the grain of sight
gives way to
sound

Walking Cautiously

on ice each step
across the lake
enlightened by care
only death creates
life we are told
leads us on

Peace

```
  ──   ──
  ── ── ──
  ─────────
  ─────────
```

begins with breath
drawn in slowly
released to arrive
where one is
known as home
she's there

Obstruction

```
  ─────────
  ─────────
  ──   ──
  ── ── ──
  ── ── ──
```

snow surrounds the lake
light blocked above
keeps us awake
to what's
in the
way

Allies

pheasant spreads her
wings cover those
who gather as snow
falls each before
the other says
I do too

Great Harvest

new snow
across the ridge
mountains rise in the east
a small fire burns below
the summit warm
enough for two

Modesty

turn north
to watch deer
through aspen
and pine each step
light as silence
loses sight

Contentment

contains itself as well
we hear hard against
ease or assent says
on the other
side she
rests

Following

the path beyond
the lake turns southeast
switchback up a ridge
in ankle deep snow
nothing below
but remains

Implosion

three days to prepare
three nights to wait
while thought doubles
back to handle
the harder one
turns in

Overseeing

from the pass
between lake and
river runs underneath
my mind holds its own
image implies much
more than itself

Viewing

so hard
her not being
here as
given
for
us

Biting Into

memory bites back
breaks skin thin
as thinking I
see thunder
first then
fire

Adorn

with white silk her
steps star us open
to change so simple
or seen from here
there isn't
so far

Freeing Yourself

from what was never
the question but how
to live without
an insistent I
hear the mind
murmur

Return

and seek the center
where we meet
not apart from but
a part of blackbirds
by the hundreds
fly home

Without Falsehood

```
═══════
═══════
══  ══
══  ══
```

come down to cross
the river and see
spring's first redbud
bloom too early
the oracle warns
too late

Great Developments

```
══  ══
══  ══
═══════
═══════
```

stark and stand
still unheard anger
or ought to be said
folds under sky hides
hill and hand safe
but not sound

Nourishment

script written on stone
thrown sticks broken
by chance feeds
on words like
air and
ash

Great Endurance

lake surface
shattered by wind
wheat fields shorn
by scythes leave
nothing behind
but bone

The Watery Depths

```
──   ──
─────────
──   ──
─── ─── ───
──   ──
```

some rice
some wine
so little left to offer
once she was
not now we
know

Illumination

```
─────────
──   ──
─────────
──   ──
─────────
```

sudden as fire burns out
nothing lasts or is lost
a pheasant flies
east at sunrise
passing in
time

Ocotober 1996—May 1997

LOWER CANON

for my father

Mutual Influence

without her
he lost his way
eight years later
so little left for him
to say 'it's all just
a big blank wall'

Constancy

who isn't what we
remember his constant
heart scattered by change
a field birds flee thunder
above wind below
no reprieve

Withdrawal

almost without
an I to weave back
to one sundered life
no oracle assigns
nor oversees this
unraveling retreat

Great Strength

where now to wander
middle-aged implicated
in my own demise
an enemy more deadly
within than without great
strength darkened fate

Advance

☷

sit on cliffs above the sea
watching waves spray
against rocks fight hard
to forget the binding
lies regret tells
of itself

Dimming Light

☲

at first a fire
of which there is
no image endures
long after this spark
struck moment fades to
fact then wind scattered ash

Household

what prevails once
the house comes down
is prevailing itself
a bark beetle feeding
on the core of a
eucalyptus tree

Contrariety

seen as complement
or adversary on either
side of eagle's ravine
asks if empty defeats
full or completes
its alternate course

Hardship

more broken lines
than whole his heart
recedes each day a little
less need for what once
looked back from the
mirror's angled eye

Relief

in rain after thunder
hovers above a choice
between not letting
go and easing
in the end
alone

Decreasing

one phrase each day
awakens another
new moon unsung
its tale untold
to stars before
darkness falls

Increasing

early sun
among aspen
trees rise up from
beneath what I see
yellow leaves
drift down

Eliminating

an I tenacious in all
its urgent forms
folds up as nothing
but now remains
of thoughts lost on
a forgotten then

Encountering

any enemy within or without
sense sequestered as reason
tears at its own wounds
open an origin that
couldn't become
any other way

Gathering

a purple heart
his brother didn't
live to see a ring his
father never wore
this rumpled
hat I have

Arising

even as anger
eludes these words
turn like leaves to lyric
debris becomes
spring's new
feast

Impasse

what blocks the way
memory wrestles
with sounds he knows
as words evade
a voice bewildered
by itself

The Well

what blocks the way

a rope too short
to reach water below
only a low tone brought
up from a bucket
knocking on
rock walls

Abolishing the Old

engrained
enemy within
emergent lure nothing
but a resonant urge
insists I remain
entangled

Establishing the New

a matter of imagining
the real as it always is
becoming more or
less than it was
in memory
alone

Taking Action

may mean
sitting quietly
legs crossed hands
overlap thumbs touch
tip to tip each breath
turns inside out

Keeping Still

waiting for what can't be
in a bed that isn't his
a return to a home
he doesn't recall
longing still
in place

Developing Gradually

from
wondering
what becomes
of what I am not
awakened only
aggrieved

Marrying Maiden

to recall
eight years
later as snow
fell we became
one to wonder why
he couldn't remember

Abundance

of other than
thinking a limit
brushed up against
or only a rumor
an absence of
grasping

Traveling

evening's early moon
pulse quick from flight
a memory of metaphor
these shadow words
bear a little known
night passing by

Yielding

or grasping
absence as light
between leaves
of a camellia tree
sign of the sun
imagined eye

Joy

still finds its way
amid day's detritus
low tide at sunset
slow walk along
the shore her
warm hand

Dispersing

```
═══════
═   ═
═   ═
═   ═
```

his
ardor
forgotten
each thought
scattered from
its own insistence

Restraint

```
─   ─
═══════
═   ═
═══════
```

no bounds but
edges reined in
by change braces
against an angle
of life hidden
in sight

Innermost Sincerity

▤

rarely without a word
to put us all at ease
humor almost
to the end
he never
feared

The Small Things

▤

a meal
shared a laugh
for no reason misses
so much left to say
so few words
suffice

Finished

step from stone
to stream with care
cross over these lines
slowly three of each
empty then full an
alternate end

Unfinished

red tailed hawk flies
west at sunset passing
nothing but time lasts
or is lost to change
begins once
again

November 2004—July 2005

LIMBIC KNIT

for Siena

Illumination

how much more than
thought this small spark
catching fire inside her
hope for good health
yet fears the end will
arrive before beginning

Mutual Influence

neither will know
the one to come she's
gone he's without a way
to recall their seed a
simple need to be
some of each

Gathering

itself as cells
grow one from
another life awaits
an uncertain world
incites this line
of descent

Withdrawal

step back from being
an I aligned only
with its own mind
unravels a miraculous
dream of the real
rumored to be true

Developing Gradually

```
═══════
  ═   ═
═══════
  ═   ═
```

and the reason
for that which needs
none holds its tongue
knows this growth
the mind defies
a body obeys

The Small Things

```
  ═   ═
═══════
═══════
  ═   ═
```

what manner of hands
unencumbered by
birth renders gesture
too small to forget
this image becomes
obsolete each day

Taking Action

there is no beyond
words stake their claim
before what isn't
here the act back of
which nothing is
on its own

Unfinished

blue sky humid day
no hawk or pheasant
flies behind her or
was it his heartbeat
we heard making
a way to be told

The Adolescent

even the answers
oracles know undermine
assent the young come
after the old see their
mistakes made again
conceded in time

Obstruction

given what
obstructs the true
rule no more than an
echo of order sounding
out the edges of a
perjured world

Contrariety

oblique
even to our
selves as others
feed on care
everyone
craves

Yielding

witnessed only as
what doesn't grasp
at life the new grows
within an absence
of light I wait
outside of

Great Developments

all possibility settles
in her changing shape
shows what's to come
another voice not yet
a voice heard as any
one's expression

Following

the familiar
distance of a face
opaque among
forms of being seen
as more than
semblance of need

Dispersing

```
━━━━━
━━  ━━
━━━  ━━
━━━━━
━━  ━━
```

goldfinch pecks
at seed leaves little
behind of what wasn't
I never thought its
scattered pattern
a sign of flight

Constancy

```
━━  ━━
━━━━━
━━━━━
━━  ━━
```

saw today it's
she not he here
on the near shore
where we wait
in change's
wake

Encountering

this matter of living
matter this mid-life
gift emerging from
cell to self her origin
in so many no other
way one becomes

Modesty

wind ripples
grand lake waits
on rain waits on
this ritual of the
new demands
no answers

Advance

scared a fox
scaring a squirrel
watched it trot off
hungry unappeased
we walk where it was
an unexpected measure

Freeing Yourself

from the need
to see mother and
child inside as one
or many opposed
or entwined each
word for word

Abolishing the Old

to set aside
the frayed ways
clinging cares for
changing forms
once again a
new skin

The Well

is where she isn't
left with empty hands
but rope to reach
water brought up
to cleanse or quench
all desire's undone

Restrain the Lesser

broken light laced
through spruce
slight shadow
casts under
standing
aside

Great Harvest

what amends
soil so abundant
her belly turns earth
fecund in decay
these signs
of life

Decreasing

```
━━━━━━━    ━━  ━━
━━  ━━     ━━  ━━
━━  ━━     ━━  ━━
━━━━━━━    ━━  ━━
```

will erodes what use
old rules retain
their pull stays behind
as habit's phantom
limb touches nothing
fills this need

Birth Pangs

```
━━  ━━     ━━  ━━
━━━━━━━    ━━  ━━
━━  ━━     ━━  ━━
━━━━━━━    ━━  ━━
```

the home
her body is
now aware no
subtle rupture
leads being
through

Disagreement

who wouldn't fear
this world she'll become
one in another's eyes
estranged as envy
measured by
demise

Abundance

of muted truth
only you two know
an inner limit with
in this instant is
anything but
absence

The Army

which must make
what isn't the same
so easily subsumed
under identity doesn't
know its own abuse
wears reason away

Eliminating

any place beyond
question a face no one
sees before birth her
smile ripe to arrive
absolves as fate
may have it

Nourishment

another
kind of music
she needs to break
from shadow's grip
this scale of light
echoes eclipse

Household

which word escapes
the allure of what isn't
given to the eye or I
believe it was home
hidden among lines
true to their reach

Peace

being called
from birth her
breath possibility's
new measure names
the old way one
comes of two

Patience

this world widens
with time crossing
over eyes barely open
to words for good
fortune patience
has as its end

Traveling

these hours I've
rarely been awake for
night passing by no
image or shadow
of truth this in
consolable cry

Viewing

does he see her as
his son's only or
any other's love
born of such
care given
to us

Contentment

arrives in circadian
cadence the sky is time
our sun marks off as
early days undefined
before words order
her emergent world

Adorn

me with ease
to be with you so
small your hands
grasp for what
isn't all that
we are

The Creative

ten years ago a poem began
sky above and sky below
the first of many to say
she's gone and now
a new one takes flight
in time says begin again

Hardship

isn't
what is
thought of
broken by
cries at
night

Establishing the New

```
  ——    ——
  ——————————
  ——————————
  ——    ——
```

which rituals
allow days to take
shape as imagined
order appears before
her eyes follow us
less than necessity

Finished

```
  ——    ——
  ——————————
  ——————————
  ——————————
```

now three
each empty then
full an alternate image
advanced in hope
old ways end
eclipsed

Marrying Maiden

so slight her smile
gathers this incipient
life around form as
wonder redundant
yet new a tenuous
antecedent least

Arising

between lines
broken and whole
one turn to the root
reveals at inception
anger assuaged by
the given isn't

Walking Cautiously

☰

on razor point trail
wondering which
white lies we'll
tell to temper
the truth un
certain as it is

Impasse

☷

what weight
the scale holds
memory informs
its impasse all
that's set
aside

Overseeing

before
meaning
assigns her
sounds ebb
and flow like
littoral drift

Biting Into

a life beginning to
sort itself as sense
arrayed in rhythms
of sound and shape
taste smell and touch
under change's sway

Dimming Light

⚌
⚍

so little
left of who
he was a great
reserve of quiet
compassion a slight
fire a pheasant flies by

Without Falsehood

⚌
⚏

I would love
truth to weigh
in and say this
is the last glass
reason holds
against me

The Watery Depths

⚏⚎
⚍⚋
⚎⚍
⚏⚏

does any
thing beneath
thinking draw words
away an undertow
she'll need to
know

Allies

⚌⚌
⚍⚍
⚎⚎
⚏⚏

this limbic knit
of memory is mind
all that gathers up
time's synaptic riff
secures sense to
its own device

The Receptive

but which are
the true objects
she receives ten
thousand things
ask her glance
rests where

Implosion

giving a little
wards off more
disease doubles
back as cure
one turns
within

Unity

is it anything
other than a weight
less faith she acts
on a vestige no
one knows
it whole

Increasing

an arc
of attention
at the margin
of what's beside
life a spark from
the empty set

Keeping Still

wondering what
accrues in sleep
an alchemy of image
and sound defines her
time we hope won't
fall to our fears

Joy

two beautiful smiles
precede these lines
teased out at low tide
watched from sand
stone rocks eroding
I share their fate

Relief

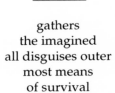

turned fifty today
first flowers in bloom
on torrey pines trail
yerba santa and sea
cliff buckwheat seen
by a fortunate man

Innermost Sincerity

gathers
the imagined
all disguises outer
most means
of survival
a sign

Return

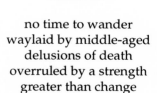

what will she make
of these words once
she can read rock rose
and black sage are back
along broken hill trail
turns toward the sea

Great Strength

no time to wander
waylaid by middle-aged
delusions of death
overruled by a strength
greater than change
gives birth to

Great Endurance

```
— —   — —
═══════
═══════
—  —   — —
```

love
the allure
of enduring
cell to cell
self to
self

Restraint

```
— —   — —
═══════
— —   — —
═══════
```

we have only begun
to see who she will
become no oracle
knows the limits
life imposes so
open ended

June 2006—March 2007

Acknowledgements

Eight of the poems in *Upper Canon* appeared in *Chicago Review*, thanks to Devin Johnston; all of *Lower Canon* appeared in *Hambone*, thanks to Nathaniel Mackey, and Quarry Press published all of *Upper Canon* as a chapbook, thanks to Andrew Mossin.

I had the great fortune to have a very astute group of readers for these poems over the eleven years of their gestation. Norman Fischer, Lindsay Hill, Hank Lazer, Andrew Mossin, and my wife, Debi Kilb, all had a hand in making this a better book. I am deeply appreciative of their attention.